G. H. C. Macgregor

The Christian's Aspirations

G. H. C. Macgregor

The Christian's Aspirations

ISBN/EAN: 9783337182212

Printed in Europe, USA, Canada, Australia, Japan

Cover: Foto ©Lupo / pixelio.de

More available books at **www.hansebooks.com**

THE

CHRISTIAN'S ASPIRATIONS

BY

THE REV. G. H. C. MACGREGOR, M.A.

AUTHOR OF "A HOLY LIFE," "PRAYING TO
THE HOLY GHOST," ETC.

NEW YORK: 46 East 14th Street

THOMAS Y. CROWELL & COMPANY

BOSTON: 100 Purchase Street

Norwood Press

J. S. Cushing & Co. — Berwick & Smith

Norwood Mass. U.S.A.

CONTENTS

CHAPTER I.

CHAPTER VIII.

THE CHRISTIAN'S ASPIRATIONS.

CHAPTER I.

THE ASPIRATION AFTER THE VISION OF GOD.

" And he said, 'I beseech Thee, show me Thy glory'" (Exod. xxxiii. 18).

THIS is the highest aspiration of the human soul. Higher than this man cannot get. All that we long for is summed up in the vision of God. When that vision in unclouded splendor breaks on a man's soul, he is already in heaven.

But this aspiration, although the highest aspiration of the soul, is found in the lowest of men. Wherever a man is found, there is a being within whom there is a simply unappeasable thirst for God. This thirst is ineradicable, being an original attribute of the soul made in the image of God.

In the unconverted, this longing for God, although present, is covered up. The affections of the unsaved cling round the things of earth. But in the regenerate, the longing for God simply flames forth. When God quickens a soul, and reveals Himself to it in any measure, He awakens in it an unquenchable longing for further revelation. The soul which has once seen God, yearns for fuller vision; for vision means knowledge, and knowledge means bliss.

5

Of this longing for the vision of God, we have many examples in Scripture. Look at Moses. Here was a man to whom God had given everything a man could desire. He had 'wisdom, knowledge, riches, and power. He had favor with God and man. But all that could not satisfy him. The cry of his life was, "I beseech Thee, show me Thy glory."

Or take the case of Job. The vision which Moses felt was necessary for *work*, Job felt was needful for *suffering*. The whole of that wonderful book is a cry for God, a cry which is only satisfied when Job can say, "Now my eye seeth Thee." Or take the book of Psalms. The deepest cry of that is the cry for the vision of God. The writer of the sixty-third Psalm expresses the feelings of all when he says: "My soul thirsteth for Thee, my flesh longeth for Thee in a dry land where no water is; to see Thy power and Thy glory, so as I have seen Thee in the sanctuary."

This vision of God after which the soul aspires is threefold : —

I. It is a vision of *the Divine Majesty*. This was what God granted to Job. He made His power to pass before Job, showing Him the Divine strength as it is manifested in the works of creation until the soul of the patriarch was overwhelmed (Job xlii. 5).

II. It is a vision of *the Divine Holiness*. This was what God granted to Isaiah. As he beheld the Lord high and lifted up, and the dazzling purity of God flashed in upon his soul, there burst from him the cry : "Woe is me, for I am undone, for I am a man of unclean lips, and dwell among a people of unclean lips, for my eyes have seen the King, the Lord of hosts" (Isa. vi. 5).

III. It is a vision of *the Divine Love.* This was what God granted to Moses. You remember that when Moses cried, "I beseech Thee, show me Thy glory," the reply of the Lord was, "I will make all *My goodness* pass before thee." The glory that Moses saw was the glory of the Divine love.

This, then, is the vision of God for which all Christian hearts are longing.

Now, THIS ASPIRATION OF THE SOUL IS ONE WHICH GOD WILL CERTAINLY SATISFY.

God sometimes hides Himself; but to the soul who is patient He will reveal Himself at last. He has not said to any one, Seek ye My face in vain. That He will reveal Himself, He gave us the assurance when He said, "Look unto Me, and be ye saved."

It was that He might satisfy this longing of the soul of man that He gave Jesus to the world. That men might see God it was needful that God should become incarnate, "No man hath seen God at any time; the Only Begotten Son, which is in the bosom of the Father, He hath declared Him." Now, He says, "He that hath seen Me hath seen the Father," and calls to us, "Behold the Lamb of God."

But if we would see God, there are certain conditions to which we must conform. They are these : —

I. *We must be in the cleft of the Rock.*

It was only after being safely hidden there, that Moses dared look upon God. Until we are reconciled to God in Jesus Christ the vision of God is impossible. "The God of this world hath blinded the minds of them that believe not." It is eyes which have been touched with the precious blood, that alone see God.

II. *We must look for God only in Jesus Christ.*

This is not an unnecessary rule. There are some most devout people who seem to use Jesus Christ as a means for getting to the Father, but who seem to think that this getting to the Father will take them past, and away from the Son. This has been the mistake of mystics in all ages. Those who fall into it show that they have never properly grasped the teaching of the Scriptures about the Deity of Jesus. The vision of God that we long for is the vision of the glory of Jesus. We are to see the Glory of God in "the face of Christ Jesus."

III. *Our eyes must be ever towards the Lord.*

Just as upon the eye that is steadfastly directed towards any part of the heavens, there breaks the vision of stars before unseen; just as upon the sensitive plate which is long exposed, there are registered stars, at first quite invisible even to it, so to the soul whose gaze is unceasingly directed toward God, there is granted a vision of His glory, of which the soul who has not learned to wait on God can know nothing.

But if these conditions are fulfilled, then the aspiration of the soul will be satisfied. The glory of the Lord will be revealed. We shall see it, and adore.

And what will be the effect on our souls? It will be fivefold : —

(1) There will be *self-condemnation.* This is the effect of the vision of the Divine Majesty. When, like Job, we see the majesty of God, we abhor ourselves, and repent in dust and ashes.

(2) There will be *self-abhorrence.* This is the effect of the vision of the Divine Holiness. When there is granted to us the vision of God, we shall be smitten to the ground, as Isaiah was.

(3) There will be *self-abasement.* This is the effect of the vision of the Divine Love. When, like Moses, we see the glory of God, we shall bow the head and worship.

(4) There will be *transfiguration.* As we behold the glory of the Lord, we shall be changed into the same image from glory to glory, by the Spirit of the Lord.

(5) There will be *satisfaction.* Joy there will be at once, with increasing knowledge, increasing joy, and at last the beatific vision. "As for me, I will behold Thy face in righteousness ; I shall be satisfied, when I awake, with Thy likeness."

CHAPTER II.

THE ASPIRATION AFTER THE FRIENDSHIP OF GOD.

" He was called the Friend of God " (Jas. ii. 23).

THE praises of Friendship have been sung in all ages of the world. In prose and poetry, its virtues have been extolled. Consequently, the definitions of it are innumerable. At one or two of these we may now look.

Plato says : "Friendship is, strictly speaking, reciprocal benevolence, which inclines each party to be solicitous for the welfare of the other, as for his own. This quality of affection is created and preserved by a similarity of disposition and manner."

Fleming says : "Friendship is the mutual esteem and regard cherished by kindred minds ; often begun, and always cemented, by the interchange of good offices."

Bishop Martensen says : "Friendship is a union between individuals, for mutual help and strength, founded not on respect alone, but on sympathy."

Friendship is a want of human nature; and the longing for friendship, which is universal, is the expression of a deep need of the human soul.

There are, in particular, *four great evils* which afflict humanity, a refuge from which is sought in friendship.

(1) The first of these is *Loneliness.* Man is a social being, and protests against being left alone. Loneliness is one of the bitterest trials of life. All of us know that the worst kind of imprisonment is solitary confinement. Those who are subjected to it for any long period invariably go mad. From the bitterness of loneliness, refuge is sought in the companionship of friends.

(2) The second evil is *Sorrow.* When a heavy bereavement falls on us, when a sore sickness distresses us, there is awakened in the human heart an inappeasable longing for sympathy. We want to tell our griefs to some one, in whose heart they will awaken a sympathetic grief. But sympathy can only be found in the heart of a friend.

(3) The third evil is *Perplexity.* Life is tangled and difficult. At times we are panic-stricken by our difficulties. We know not how to act, the perplexity is maddening, and we long for advice. We long to have some one to whom we can submit our case, and whom we can trust to give us the aid of his wisdom. But this we can find only in a friend.

(4) The fourth evil is *Weakness.* At times dangers will threaten us which we cannot avoid, and blows will fall which quite disable us. Then we need more than advice or sympathy; we need succor, and only from our friends can we get it.

These are the evils, great and terrible, for which friendship supplies the remedy. A friend's companionship will remove loneliness; a friend's sympathy will lighten sorrow; a friend's advice will remove perplexity; and, ofttimes, a friend's succor will save us from ruin.

But, while human friendship can do so much, there constantly arise situations in life where the best of earthly friends fail. By the call of duty, or by death, our friends may be removed from us, and we be deprived of their companionship; sorrows may fall on us too deep for them to fathom, and their sympathy be utterly vain; perplexities may arise which they are powerless to unravel, and difficulties may come in presence of which they are as weak as ourselves.

So there arises a longing for a companionship that will never be broken, for a sympathy that will never misunderstand, for a wisdom that will never be baffled, for a strength that will never fail. This longing is the cry of the human heart for the friendship of God.

This longing, which is found in all hearts, becomes perfectly definite and conscious in the heart of the Christian. Now, what is the path which leads to the friendship of God?

We shall be able to answer this question by noticing what are the conditions of any true friendship.

(1) In order to friendship there must be *community of nature*. It is only by a use of metaphor that we speak of the dog as the friend of man. Friendship implies kinship of nature. Therefore, if we would be the friends of God, we must become " partakers of the Divine nature." And this we can only become through being born again.

(2) There must be *community of feeling*. A man may love those who do not love him, but friendship is mutual. If we are to be the friends of God, God's love to us

must be met by a responsive love. But this implies reconciliation. For we do not naturally love God. We are aliens and enemies in our minds by wicked works. It is at the cross of Jesus Christ, where He has reconciled all thing unto Himself, that the sinful soul enters on the friendship of God.

(3) There must be *perfect trust*. Where there is suspicion friendship cannot live. Unless we are ready to believe that our God will never do for us less than the very best, the true bliss of His friendship cannot be ours.

(4) There must be *obedience*. This is not necessary for an earthly friendship, but it is absolutely necessary for the soul that would know the friendship of God. Jesus Christ has told us quite distinctly: " Ye are My friends, if ye do whatsoever I command you " (John xv. 14).

These, then, are the conditions of the Divine friendship. If we fulfil them, how bright the glory that will burst upon our souls! There will be given to us a companionship which will never be broken, a sympathy which will never fail, a wisdom to which all things are clear, and a strength to which all things are easy.

But, in addition to these blessings, there are others into which the Divine friendship introduces us. These we can only mention in a word.

(*a*) There is *a knowledge of the Divine counsels* (Gen. xviii. 17 ; John xv. 15). When we become the friends of God, He reveals to us the things which He is about to do.

(*b*) There is *a vision of the Divine glory* (Exod. xxxiii. 17).

(*c*) There is *a share in the Divine work ;* and, finally,

(*d*) There is *a likeness to the Divine person*. The vision of God in glory is the climax of spiritual bliss. And we are told we shall be like Him, when we see Him as He is.

CHAPTER III.

THE ASPIRATION AFTER WALKING WITH GOD.

"Enoch walked with God" (Gen. v. 24).

THIS aspiration of the soul is one which naturally follows that which we last considered. It is he who knows something of the friendship of God, who aspires to walk with God. For walking with God is one of the most blessed characteristics of the life of friendship.

Of only three of the Old Testament saints is it expressly said that they walked with God. But though the phrase is only used of Enoch, Noah, and Levi, the experience was by no means confined to them. Abraham knew what it was to walk with God, and it was with God beside him that he made his way from Ur of the Chaldees to the land of the promise. Moses knew this experience, and it was the presence of God with him that nerved him for the almost superhuman task to which he was called. David knew it, and it was with God beside him that he rose to the throne of Israel. And the experience which these enjoyed has been the experiences of countless thousands of men and women through all the ages.

But what is meant by walking with God ? It is not an act, nor yet a series of acts, but a condition of life consistently maintained through years. Enoch, we are told, walked with God three hundred years. Walking with God was no exceptional experience with him. It was the normal condition of his life. So it should be with us. Our whole life, the daily life which is apt to be so monotonous, is meant to be lived in quiet calm fellowship with God. Life is not made up of rapture. Rapturous experiences can only be occasional. But in the daily round of life we are meant to walk with God.

If you ask me what is the chief characteristic of the man who is walking with God, I reply, his continual consciousness of God. It is in this that the heart of the matter consists. Of the man who walks with God it may be said that the thought of God is never out of his mind. He is always conscious of God, or I would prefer to say *sub-conscious.* He lives in God as in the atmosphere.

But how is this experience to be ours ?

This walk, like all walks, must have A STARTING POINT, A DIRECTION, and A GOAL. At these we shall briefly look.

I. THE STARTING POINT IS THE CROSS.

Fellowship with God for sinners is possible only on the basis of atonement. It is by the blood of Jesus that we have access to the presence of God. How wonderful it is to turn to the Scriptures to see what we owe to the lood. In Exodus, Moses tells us of deliverance through the blood (Exodus xii. 13); in the Pauline Epistles we read of pardon, justification, peace, access through the blood. Peter tells us of redemption, John of cleansing, the Apocalypse of victory, and all through the blood. He who is not washed in the blood will never walk with God, and the walk cannot be continued if for a moment the power of the blood is forgotten. God waits at the cross to meet the sinner, and from that point only can the walk with God begin.

II. The Direction is the Line of the Will of God.

The path in which we walk with God is the path of God's commandments. The Christian's desire must never be that God should go his way, but ever that he should go God's way. The Christian should desire, not so much always to have God with him, as always to be with God. It is most instructive to see how intense this desire was in the heart of the Psalmist. In Psalm after Psalm we have the cry, " Teach me Thy way," " Make me to run in the path of Thy commandments, for I delight therein." God keeps ever in the line of His will, and if we would walk with Him, we must keep there also. We lose God when we gain our own way. How true this is, the histories of Abraham and Balaam teach us.

III. The Goal of the Walk is a Life which may be described as having none of self, and all of God.

This is beautifully brought out in the story of Enoch. There we read that " Enoch walked with God, *and was not.*" By the consciousness of God, the consciousness of self is gradually extinguished. That death to self, for which so many long, is a consequence of fellowship with God. When we walk with God, our life becomes one of which we can say, " It is not I that live; but Christ liveth in me." Nothing but the continual consciousness of God will effect this. It is something brought about not by effort and strain, but by restful trust. And what a change it makes ! The "I" hot-tempered, proud, foolish, disobedient, deceived, envious, hateful and hating others, gives place to the " Christ" meek, lowly, obedient, self-denying, and loving. So we die to self, and live to God.

But in the story of Enoch, we read that he was not,
" for God took him." This reminds us that the God who
led him out of a life the centre of which was self, led
him into a life of joy and courage and unbroken peace.
Thus he was fitted for that which was the crown of his
life, his translation into the presence of the Lord.

For us who live so far down the stream of time how
great the significance of this fact! It shows us that the
life that walks with God is a life, I do not say ready for
death, but ready for translation. Are you walking with
God ? Then you also, like Enoch, are ready to be trans-
lated. Of how many of us is this true ? How many of
us are ready for the coming of the Lord ? It is near us
now, and coming nearer every day. May God help us
all so to walk with Him that we shall look for and
hasten unto the coming of our Lord, and to His promise,
" Behold, I come quickly," answer with the prayer,
" Even so, come, Lord Jesus."

CHAPTER IV.

THE ASPIRATION AFTER DELIGHT IN GOD'S WILL.

" I delight to do Thy will, O my God " (Psalms xl. 8).

"IT is very hard, but I suppose I must put up with it,
seeing it is the will of God." This is the language which
is only too frequently heard on the lips of God's children.
If we have not all used it, we have all had the feelings
which the words express. It is because we feel that we
ought to rejoice in God's will, yet know that we do not
rejoice in it, that the prayer for delight in the will of
God is so frequently and earnestly offered.

That a Christian should not rejoice in his Father's will is sad; but it is hardly to be wondered at. God is so mysterious. He is constantly doing things which seem arbitrary, and He rarely explains Himself.

His *delays* are mysterious — at times, maddening. He lets our Lazarus die before our eyes, when it seems to us that if He had hastened but a little He might have saved us from our sorrow. We cry in our pain, " Lord, if Thou hadst been here, our brother had not died "; but Jesus comes not to raise our Lazarus, and as we weep over our dead we say sadly, " The will of the Lord be done."

Then the *movements* of God are as mysterious as His delays. How often when we thought we had come to a quiet resting-place, He has stirred us up, and sent us out to meet pain and sorrow.

It is these things, and things like them, that make us feel that we do not delight in God's will, and make us aspire so earnestly after true joy in it. Now let us lay to heart, *this is an aspiration which may be fulfilled.* It is possible for us to delight in the will of God. It is possible for us *always* to delight in the will of God.

This was the experience of our Lord Jesus Christ. He could always say, " I delight to do Thy will, O my God; yea, Thy law is within my heart." And He has told us that as He was so are we to be in this world.

Then this experience was enjoyed by many of the Old Testament saints. Look, for example, at the writer of Psalm cxix. There was a man who found the deepest delight of his life in the will of God. His whole Psalm is a hymn of praise to the will of God, and in every verse of it there is a reference to the will of God, either as law, or testimony, or precept, or statute, or word. In the twenty-fourth verse he expressly says, " Thy testimonies are my delight."

And this experience is enjoyed by many round about us. Not long ago I met a man who said to me, "I have come from long experience of the will of God so to rejoice in it, that if God said to me, Go, lie down on the road and die, I would do it with the greatest pleasure. I cannot conceive anything so delightful as the will of God." Another said to me, "For years I have let God manage my life, and He has done it so well that I would never dream of taking it out of His hands."

These men were not boasting. Both of them are among the humblest men I have ever met. They were just confessing what all who give themselves up to do the will of God confess — that in the will of God is the purest source of human joy.

But if this experience is attainable, how are we to attain it? For the attainment of it, I think the following rules may be helpful.

(1) *Settle it in your mind that the will of God is always good*, and that, therefore, it is a *reasonable* thing to delight in it. Delight is, no doubt, a matter of the affections rather than of the reason, but to convince the reason of the righteousness of any feeling is a great help towards the awakening of that feeling. When I say that we ought to convince ourselves that the will of God is good, I virtually say that we ought to take pains to know the will of God. If I study the will of God as it is revealed in the Bible, I can scarcely help falling in love with it. Why! what is the will of God? For those that are lost? "As I live, saith the Lord, I have no pleasure in the death of the wicked, but that the wicked turn from his evil way, and live" (Ezek. xxxiii. 11). "This is the will of Him that sent Me, that every one that seeth the Son, and believeth on Him, may have everlasting life" (John

vi. 40). For those that are saved? "Fear not, little flock, it is the Father's good pleasure to give you the Kingdom." "This is the Father's will which hath sent Me, that of all which he hath given Me I should lose nothing, but raise it up again at the last day" (John vi. 39). "This is the will of God, even your sanctification" (1 Thess. iv. 3). "In everything give thanks, for this is the will of God in Christ Jesus concerning you" (1 Thess. v. 18). In the will of God there is everything of blessing for His people. If we really knew, as we may know from His Word, what God wills, we should not find it hard to say "Thy will be done."

(2) *Remember that there is within you a principle of life which makes it easy for you to delight in the will of God.*

This was given you in regeneration. Previously there was within you a carnal heart, which was at enmity against God, and an evil heart of unbelief, which departed from the Living God. But now, being in Christ, you are new creatures, with a new love ruling your life. You can now say, "I delight in the law of God after the inward man." The nature of the new life given to you is such, that as a flower turns to the sun, so you turn to God. It is natural for your new nature to rejoice in God's will. Let your new nature have scope. Yield it up to the Holy Spirit, that He may fill it, and He will give you such a vision of the glory of God's will as will ravish your soul.

(3) *Give yourself up in all circumstances, and at all times, to do the will of God.*

After all, the secret of delighting in God's will is to do it. Only when it is accepted and carried out does the joy it leads to become ours. Obedience, which is the path of knowledge, is also the path of gladness. When a man is determined to do the will of God, whether he likes it or not, he soon finds in it a source of unfailing joy, until at last he can come to sing words like these : —

> Thou sweet, beloved will of God.
>   My anchor ground, my fortress hill,
> My spirit's silent fair abode,
>   In Thee I hide me, and am still.
>
> Thy wonderful grand will, my God,
>   With triumph now I make it mine ;
> And faith shall cry a joyous Yes !
>   To every dear command of Thine.

CHAPTER V.

THE ASPIRATION AFTER LOVE OF GOD'S WORD.

"Thy Word is very pure ; therefore Thy servant loveth it" (Psalm cxix. 140).

ALL of us have often read the 119th Psalm, and all of us must often in our secret hearts have envied the writer of it. For he was a man in whose case the aspiration we are now considering was fulfilled in quite an unusual degree. That man had a perfect passion for the Word of God. In his wonderful Psalm every verse is devoted to the praise of God's Word. This man could never get over the fact that God should have revealed Himself at all. It is to him matter of constant adoration and praise. Therefore, he naturally delights in the revelation God had given. See how this comes out in the Psalm. At the beginning he confesses, "Thy Word have I hid in my heart, that I might not sin against Thee." A little

later comes the verse, " I trust in Thy Word." As he
reaches the middle of the Psalm he exclaims, " Thy Word
is a lamp to my feet, and a light to my path "; while, as
he nears the close of his Psalm, he cries aloud, " I rejoice
at Thy Word, as one that findeth great spoil." Here
was a man who, though his Bible was small, esteemed it
more than his necessary food.

With many of us how different it is ! We have often
to complain of a lack of real interest in the Bible. We
read it, of course, and we urge others to read it. But we
have no deep delight in the reading of it. Some of us
love non-religious books better than the Bible. Judged
by the time we give to them, the newspaper, the novel,
the book of travel, are of more importance in our eyes
than the Word of God. Even if we will not acknowledge
that we regard them as more important, we have to
acknowledge that we find them more interesting. To
the books of the world we go spontaneously, while to the
Book of God we have to be drawn by a sense of duty.

And some of us love books about the Bible more than
the Bible itself. To put the use of devotional manuals
in place of the study of the Word of God is one of the
subtlest dangers to which an earnest Christian is exposed. He who tries to nourish his soul on man's
thoughts about the Word of God, will find himself
starved. Yet this is what thousands habitually do.

However, we do study the Bible. Most of us are prob-
ably members of one or other of those Scripture Unions,
which have done such incalculable good in promoting
the reading of God's Word. We read the Bible, but we
find it very dry. It is so distressingly familiar. We
know what is coming, and our minds wander in spite
of ourselves. Like the Israelites in the wilderness, we

feel inclined to cry, " Give us something new to eat, for
our souls loathe this manna."

This distaste for the Word of God is a real and pain-
ful fact in the experience of many of God's people.
They know it and bewail it, and cry out for deliverance
from it. *Whence comes this evil, and how may it be cured?*

(1) Our lack of appetite for our heavenly food may be
due to *something in ourselves.*

Lack of appetite is always regarded by physicians as
a symptom of illness. If the general state of our spiritual life is low, if we are living out of fellowship with
God, or living in worldliness and self-indulgence, no
wonder if we have little love for the Word of God. If
there is some one with whom we have a quarrel, and
whom we will not forgive; if there is some plain duty
which we will not perform, — no wonder that we fear the
Bible. If this be so, let us remember there is no path
to love of the Bible except through the blood that cleanses
from all sin. We must make full confession of our sin,
we must heartily renounce it, we must surrender ourselves to God. And when He has received us, and
restored our spiritual health, with returning health will
come returning appetite.

(2) But our lack of appetite for the Word of God may
be due, not so much to spiritual sickness, as to *the manner
in which we take our food.* Good food badly served may
nauseate a healthy and hungry man.

I believe that false methods of reading and studying
the Bible have much to do with the prevailing lack of
interest in it. We study our Bibles mechanically, we
tramp monotonously along the beaten paths, and then
complain of want of freshness. The fault is not in the
Bible, but in us, who do not give it a fair chance.

The following practical rules may now be given to help us to a deeper love of the Word of God. If we would love our Bible : —

(*a*) *Let us study it regularly.*

We should not forget that the love of God's Word is an acquired taste. If we cease to use it, we cease to relish it. That we find the study of it dry, must not deter us from continuing our study, for the Bible sometimes will yield its sweetness only to the man who beats it out. There is need of importunity in Bible reading, as well as in prayer. Let us, then, study regularly and patiently, and we shall be richly rewarded.

(*b*) *Let us vary our methods of studying the Bible.*

This is one of the best ways for securing that our Bible-reading shall be always fresh. When we have got all we can get by working along one line, let us take another. At one time we may take the Bible *telescopically*. We may take a book at a time and endeavor to grasp its message. We may run rapidly through its chapters, not so much to see what they individually contain as to see what is the impression the book taken as a whole makes upon us.

At another time we may take the Bible *microscopically*. Instead of occupying ourselves with books, we may occupy ourselves with words. This is a profoundly interesting method of study, and the more it is followed, the deeper does the conviction sink into the mind of the plenary inspiration of God's holy Word. This method at its best is only open to those who know the original Bible languages, but with the aid of a book like Strong's "Exhaustive Concordance" much may be done by the English reader. As an example of this method, we might take the word "help." In the New Testament, seven words are employed to denote the idea of help, and the usage of them is so exact, that in no case could one of them be put for the other without a loss of power. The same method of study applied to the words for " sin," or the words for "prayer," yields most remarkable results.

Again, we may read the Bible *chronologically.* We may subordinate everything for the time to getting an accurate idea of the development of God's revelation of Himself. It will give a fresh interest to our reading of the Bible to trace the order in which the great truths of revelation were revealed.

Or we may read the Bible *topically.* We may go through book after book, or writer after writer, to find what each has taught on the great subjects which the Bible brings before us.

There is almost an unlimited number of ways in which the Bible may be treated, and each, as it is taken up in turn, will give a fresh interest to our reading.

(c) *Turn the Bible into prayer.*

This is a most important rule. When used in this way, the Bible becomes an amazing help to the growth of our spiritual life. It is hard not to be interested in a Scripture narrative, if while reading it we are praying God to work it out again in our own souls.

But, above all, if you would have a genuine love for the word of God,

(d) *Depend upon the Holy Ghost to make the Bible living and fresh to you.* As our failures in prayer are largely due to our forgetfulness of the special work which the Holy Ghost is ready to do for us in prayer, so our failure in Bible reading is often due to a similar cause. The Word of God without the Spirit of God will always be dry and powerless. Just as the joy of prayer is only known when we pray in the Holy Ghost, so the true joy of feeding on the Word is known only by those who give themselves up to be led by the Holy Ghost into all truth. If our daily reading of the Scriptures were always preceded by a prayer for the help of the Spirit, and by the taking up of an attitude of reliance on the Spirit, we should not have to complain of that lack of interest which troubles so many. We should rejoice in God's Word, as one that finds great spoil.

CHAPTER VI.

THE ASPIRATION AFTER POWER IN PRAYER.

" As a prince thou hast power with God " (Gen. xxxii. 28).

In the twelfth chapter of his First Epistle to the Corinthians, the Apostle Paul bids us to "covet earnestly the best gifts." In no way can we better fulfil his command than by coveting power in prayer. For assuredly it is one of God's best gifts to man. Than this there is nothing that brings more glory to God, or more blessing to human souls. And it is essentially a *grace*, a gift of God. We cannot work it in ourselves. To some men God gives it in a marvellous degree. To them prayer is a calling. It is the direction in which they are specially called to serve God. But while some of God's saints have a vocation in regard to prayer, all are bound to learn to wield this instrument, which God in His infinite grace has put into their hands.

Power in prayer means power to use prayer for the purposes for which God has given it to us. Prevailing prayer is prayer that secures answers. But this means prayer that conforms to the Divinely appointed conditions. What these are we now proceed to discover. An examination of them will show that true prayer, instead of being an easy thing, is in reality a thing most difficult, and will explain to us why our prayers have so often failed. The teaching of Scripture in regard to the conditions of prayer is so ample that we shall not be able to present it fully, but we shall look at those conditions which are the most important.

(1) The first condition is *Heart Separation from sin.*

"If I regard iniquity in my heart, the Lord will not hear me" (Psalm lxvi. 18). "The sacrifice of the wicked is an abomination to the Lord" (Prov. xv. 8). Consecration to God and holiness of life are necessary to prevailing prayer. A heart that loves sin, a life that is spent for self, are fatal hindrances to prayer. No doubt, as the writer of the sixty-sixth Psalm expressly tells us, God in His mercy hears and answers the prayers of very unsanctified people, but such do not wield the power in prayer of which we are now speaking. He who ascends into the hill of God, and stands in His holy place, must have clean hands and a pure heart.

(2) The second condition is *Righteousness.* This we are told by the Apostle James, when he says, "The supplication of *a righteous man* availeth much" (Jas. v. 16). But what is implied in that righteousness which is needful to powerful prayer? It implies a recognition that this universe is a moral universe, a universe in which moral considerations are superior to all others. It implies a mind in sympathy with the purpose of God in the management of His universe. In particular, it implies a recognition of the absolute supremacy of God, a recogni-

tion of His absolute sovereignty, and a total self-surrender to His will. This, when combined with a recognition of the Divine grace, puts the soul in a position in which it can pray with power.

(3) The third condition is *Faith*.

"He that cometh to God must *believe* that He is." Obviously, the atheist cannot pray. "And that He is a rewarder of them that diligently seek Him" (Heb. xi. 6). Obviously, also, the deist and the agnostic cannot pray. Prayer without some measure of hope cannot exist. The Divine law in this matter is, "According to your faith be it unto you"; therefore he who would prevail in prayer must ever pray, "Lord, increase our faith."

(4) The fourth condition is *Intelligence*.

God's service is ever a reasonable service. There is nothing arbitrary or magical in God. He never outrages the reason which He has implanted in man. He often does things which transcend our reason, but He never does things which contradict it. So while He gives to us the power of prayer, He tells us it can only be exercised "according to His will." "This is the confidence that we have in Him, that if we ask anything according to His will, He heareth us" (1 John v. 14). If we are to know His will we must search for it where it is made known to us. The aspiration after power in prayer is closely connected with the aspiration after love of God's Word, for it is only when we search the Scriptures that we are able always to pray according to the mind of God.

(5) The fifth condition is *Earnestness*.

This we learn from Jer. xxix. 13, "Ye shall seek Me, and find Me, when ye shall search for Me *with all your heart*." In many of our prayers it is but too evident that we care little whether the prayer is answered or not.

Such prayer cannot prevail. God will not be mocked by a hollow approach. The value of fasting, which in many places in Scripture is connected with prayer, consists in the evidence of earnestness which it supplies. Only on the wings of strong desire can prayer reach the throne of God.

(6) Akin to earnestness is *Importunity*, which is the next condition we mention. Importunity is just continued earnestness. Its value in prayer we may judge from the fact that our Lord has given us two parables to illustrate its power. Importunity is the spirit of the wrestling Jacob (Gen. xxxii. 26) and of the Lord's remembrancers, who are to keep not silence, and to give Him no rest, till He establish, and till He make Jerusalem a praise in the earth (Isa. lxii.).

(7) The seventh condition is *Agreement with the people of God.* This is a most important, but often forgotten, condition. It applies not only to public or common prayer, but also to private or secret prayer. Our Lord said, " *If two of you shall agree* on earth as touching anything that they shall ask, it shall be done for them of my Father which is in heaven " (Matt. xviii. 19). This shows us that if we are to prevail in prayer we must pray with and for all saints, and be careful to live in love towards all the people of God. An unloving spirit, a spirit that seldom gives itself up to intercession, will never be strong in prayer. It is where brethren dwell together in unity that the Lord commands his blessing, even life for evermore (Psalm cxxxiii.).

8. As an eighth condition we may mention *Thankfulness.*

In many passages of Scripture the lesson is taught us that if we would learn to pray we must also learn to praise. To the unthankful God cannot give his best gifts. It was praise that filled the temple with the glory of God (2 Chron. v., 13); it was praise that shook the prison of Philippi to its foundations (Acts xvi. 25). And in Phil. iv. 6, where we have explicit directions about prayer, we are enjoined to combine with it thanksgiving.

Two other conditions may be noticed ere we close.

(9) If our prayer is to prevail, it must be *in the name of Jesus.* What this means is not always realized. It means far more than the use of the name of Jesus at the end of our prayers. It means not only that we recognize Jesus as the Mediator through whom we come, but that we are in such sympathy with His purposes that He can endorse our requests. This is the great secret of prevailing prayer: "If ye ask anything *in My name,* I will do it" (John xiv. 14).

(10) If our prayer is to prevail, it must be *in the Holy Ghost.* The importance of this condition is often overlooked. But true power in prayer will never be ours until, as we pray, we are upborne by the Spirit. As He teaches us what to pray for, and how to pray, our prayers will prevail, and we shall see abundant answers coming forth from the presence of God.

CHAPTER VII.

THE ASPIRATION AFTER THE FIRE OF LOVE.

"We love Him because He first loved us" (1 John iv. 19).

THAN this aspiration there is none holier or better. If we read the biographies of the saints we shall find none

more common. God is so worthy of our love. His deal-
ings with us are so marvellous. For His mercy we can
make no return but the return of love, and we feel that
the return we do make is terribly inadequate. It is the
burden of gratitude resting on our hearts that begets the
cry for the fire of love.

> " Yet I love Thee and adore —
> Oh for grace to love Thee more."

What a wonderful thing the fire of love is ! It is the
life of the soul. As Dr. Matheson says, in that remarkable little book of his, "My Aspirations," "The only
thing which is not consumed by burning is my soul.
Fire is the death of my body, but fire is the life of my
soul. When my goods are burned they perish, but when
my soul takes fire it for the first time begins to live. It
is the want of fire that consumes my soul. I want something to lift me out of myself in order that I may be
strong. Nothing can lift me out of myself but fire, the
fire of the heart — love." But many of us have to confess that this love is what is most lacking in our life.
We are not consumed by this holy flame. We are dead
and cold, even when we hate ourselves for this coldness.
Hence the strength of our aspiration, Hence the agony
of our prayers. Now how shall we get this flame kindled
in our hearts ? How shall we deal with the already
kindled flame that it may burn more brightly and hotly ?
Our love to God, we must ever remember, is the
answer of God's love to us. The apostle taught us this
when he said, "We love Him because He first loved us."
To quote Dr. Matheson again : "In Thee, O Lord, let
my heart be kindled ! Thy love alone can wake my love.
Thy fire alone can impart fire to *me*. Thy light alone

can illuminate and warm me with that ardor which consumes not." To remember that we love God in exact proportion to our recognition of the Love of God to us, is to step into the path where the fulfilment of this aspiration awaits us.

Three things may now be mentioned which act as FUEL TO THE FIRE OF LOVE. The first of these is :

(1) *Recollection.*

When our Lord Jesus Christ instituted the Lord's Supper, and said, " This do in remembrance of Me," He took the best means possible for keeping His people's love to Him alive and strong. He meant that from time to time they should pause to consider how much they owed Him, and how deeply He had loved them. He knew that could not be done without fanning into a flame their love to Him. The Lord's Supper is, as we all know, much more than a memorial; but one of the ways in which it ministers to our growth in grace is by the stimulus it gives to recollection.

If we would have the fire of love burning within us, we must give ourselves to recollection. We must gather round the cradle at Bethlehem, and as we see the Child there, we must say, " The Word was made flesh, and dwelt among us, and we beheld His glory, the glory as of the Only Begotten of the Father, full of grace and truth " (John i. 14). We must read the story of His life, until we are fascinated by it, and exclaim, " God anointed Him with the Holy Ghost and with power; who went about doing good, and healing those who were oppressed by the devil." We must go to Calvary, and look upon the Lamb of God taking away the sin of the world. We must look upon Him whom we have pierced until the greatness of His love to us overwhelms us.

We must raise our thoughts to the throne, where He is engaged in unceasing intercession for us, and our eyes to the clouds on which He will so soon be seen appearing; and as we deal with these *facts*, we shall find in them the fuel for the fire of love.

But while recollection will supply the fuel, it will not always kindle it.   This is done by —

(2) *Contemplation.*

Recollection is needful to bring the facts before our minds, contemplation is needful to make them sink into our minds.   Recollection will bring us to Bethlehem, but it is contemplation which will make us bring forth our gold, frankincense, and myrrh, as we adore Him who lies there.   Recollection will make us see the beauty of the life of Christ, but contemplation alone will teach us its meaning and its redeeming power.   But above all, it is by contemplation that the true meaning of the Cross becomes plain to us.   It is when, like those of old, we "sit down, and watch Him there"; when we take time to measure the love of which the Cross speaks, that the fire of love begins to burn in our hearts.

> "Bearing shame and scoffing rude,
> In my place condemned He stood,
> Sealed my pardon with His blood,
>   Hallelujah!"

How truly the Divine love is the fire that kindles our love we can hardly know, until we have given ourselves up to this exercise of contemplation.   As we behold the love of God, as we adore it, and rejoice in it, it descends into our hearts, and wakes them into the fervor of burning zeal.   The love of God is shed abroad in our hearts by the Holy Ghost, and we indeed love Him who first loved us.

What recollection begins, and contemplation continues, is further carried on by —

(3) *Confession.*

"We have known and believed," says the apostle John, "the love that God hath for us" (1 John iv. 16). But he had previously said, "That which we have seen and heard declare we unto you" (1 John i. 3). When we confess the love of God, and tell what we know of it; when we tell what God has done for our souls, then these things become more real to us, and prove their power in our lives. There is no surer way of making God's love unreal to us, and of quenching our love to Him, than refusing to confess him before men. When we are endeavoring to make the hearts of others burn within them by the recital of the love of Christ, it is certain that our own hearts will begin to glow. The man who says, "Come near, ye that fear God, I will declare what He hath done for my soul," will also be able to say, "I love the Lord."

But we must remember that, after all, it is not we who make ourselves love God intensely. That is the work of the Holy Ghost. He it is who sheds the love of God abroad in our hearts, and kindles within us this sacred flame. While, therefore, we remember, reflect, repeat, we must also *rely*. Trust the Holy Spirit to do this work in you, and to you will be given the joy of having a heart aflame with the love of God.

CHAPTER VIII.

THE ASPIRATION AFTER A CONTENTED SPIRIT.

" Be content with such things as ye have" (Heb. xiii. 5).

" Now, as they were going along, and talking, they espied a boy feeding his father's sheep. The boy was in very mean clothes, but of a very fresh and well-favored countenance; and as he sat by himself, he sang. Hark. said Mr. Great-heart, to what the shepherd boy saith. So they hearkened, and he said : —

' He that is down needs fear no fall ; he that is low no pride ;
He that is humble ever shall have God to be his Guide.
I am content with what I have, little it be or much ;
And, Lord, contentment still I crave, because Thou savest such.
Fulness to such a burden is, that go on pilgrimage ;
Here little, and hereafter bliss, is best from age to age.' "

So writes Bunyan, in one of the most beautiful pictures of his marvel-book. And in the praise of contentment, he is joined by every experimental writer worth naming. All feel that this is one of the best of Christian graces. One, Jeremy Taylor, in his priceless treatise "Holy Living," says, "God has appointed one remedy for all the evils in the world, and that is a contented spirit. The man who is contented nothing can hurt. Do riches come to him ? It is well. Do they take wings, and fly away ? It is well also. Is he in health ? It is well. Does sickness fall on him ? It is well also.

A contented spirit is the best equipment a man can have for facing life. He who could send his son into the world possessed of a contented spirit, would do more to secure his happiness than if he gave him all the wealth of South Africa. This is what Paul found after a long experience. He had not known it at first. God had to teach it to him, but he regarded it as one of the most valuable lessons of his life. "I have learned in whatsoever state I am therewith to be content. I know how to be abased, and I know how to abound; everywhere, and in all things, I am instructed both how to be full and to be hungry, both to abound and suffer need" (Phil. iv. 12). This statement of Paul tells us something about contentment which it is of the greatest importance for us to learn. It tells us that contentment is a habit of mind. It was something which Paul had to *learn*. It cost him effort; it cost him time. At every stage the natural discontentedness had to be overcome. If Paul had to learn it, how much more have we. How it is to be learned, it is our duty now to discover.

For cultivating the habit of content the following suggestions may be found helpful: —

(1) When tempted to murmur, *never compare your condition with that of those above you, but always with that of those beneath you.* Are you complaining of the straitness of your lot? Go and visit the really poor. When you see a condition compared with which yours is one of affluence, you will cease to murmur, and begin to praise. Wealth is a relative thing, and if we measure our desires by our condition, and not our condition by our desires, it will help us greatly in the securing of a contented spirit. "It is a huge folly," says Jeremy Taylor, "rather to grieve for the good of others, than to rejoice for that good which God has given us of our own."

(2) When tempted to murmur, *consider how much better your case is than it might have been.* To quote Jeremy Taylor again, "The very privative blessings which we

commonly enjoy, deserve the thanksgiving of a whole
life. Thou art quit of a thousand calamities, every one
of which, if it were upon thee, would make thee insensi-
ble of thy present sorrow." The habit of thanking God
for what has not happened is a most helpful one. We
have the example of the Psalmist to guide us here. In
the 103d Psalm we have no sweeter strain than that in
which the Psalmist sings, " He hath not dealt with us
after our sins ; nor rewarded us according to our iniquities. " To read what *is*, in the light of what might have
been, is one of the paths to a contented spirit.

(3) When tempted to murmur, *remember that God is at
work upon your life*, making it after His pattern, and that
He has ordered all your circumstances in accordance with
His purpose. All things are not merely for good, but for
the best. If we are the Lord's, and have really put ourselves into his His hands for the fulfilment of His will,
nothing can go wrong. Any change would be a change
for the worse. No doubt it may not seem so. But it is
so, and it is the privilege of faith to say it. That my
circumstances are so different from those of others, that
they are so much more trying, is no evidence that I am
worse placed than they. God does not intend to make
me the same as any one else, or He would have made my
circumstances the same. They are the chisels He uses
in hewing the statue, and He will use the best fitted for
His purpose. When we remember that our God is
almighty and all-loving, how unreasonable does all mur-
muring appear ! To complain of our lot is as foolish as
to complain that God made us men, and not angels or stars.

(4) But the supreme secret of content is *to have the
mind set on God*. We are restless till we reach Him.
He is the centre of all life, and the point of perfect rest.

When we are able to say with the Psalmist, " Whom have I in heaven but Thee, who is there on earth whom I desire beside Thee ? " — when God is our all in all, then this blessed secret has been learned. Nothing can then disturb our peace. For we are more taken up with the Giver than with any of His gifts. And if the gifts are removed, we remember that nothing can remove the Giver. So in the greatest straits we can rejoice, like that poor woman, who, sitting down to a crust of bread and a cup of cold water, gave thanks in the words, " All this, and God too."

CHAPTER IX.

THE ASPIRATION AFTER POWER TO REDEEM THE TIME.

" Redeeming the time " (Eph. v. 16).

" So teach us to number our days, that we may apply our hearts unto wisdom " (Psa. xc. 12). Here is the prayer of a man who aspired after power to redeem the time! He felt the moral value of time. He knew that God had given us but a short time on earth, but that on the right use of that time eternity depends. He felt also the exceeding difficulty of redeeming the time. So, in his helplessness, he casts himself on God. " So teach us to number our days, that we may apply our hearts unto wisdom."

There were three facts of life which impressed this Psalmist, and which should impress us with the urgency of making a right use of our time : —

(1) *He saw that life is short.*

To this writer, old as he was, man appeared like a

bubble on the stream. He had himself seen a whole generation swept away. So he cries, "Thou carriest them away as with a flood; they are as asleep: in the morning they are like grass that groweth up. In the morning it flourisheth and groweth up; in the evening it is cut down and withereth" (Psa. xc. 5).

And we, too, see that life is short. Year hurries after year, and not a year passes in which we have not to lay to rest those who are dear to us. Our experience confirms the word of the Apostle James, who says, "What is your life? It is even as a vapor which appeareth for a little while, and then vanisheth away" (Jas. iv. 14).

(2) *He saw that life is sorrowful.*

Short as life is, it is full of trouble. Sickness, pain, sorrow, and care pursue man from the cradle to the grave. "The days of our years are three score years and ten; and if by reason of strength they be four score, yet is their strength labor and sorrow; for it is soon cut off, and we fly away" (Psa. xc. 10).

We, too, see that life is sorrowful. Our world is not less troubled than that in which the Psalmist lived. The squalor, poverty, and wretchedness around us are such as sometimes fill us with dismay.

(3) *He saw that life is sinful.*

In this lies the explanation of the shortness and the sorrowfulness of human life. "We are consumed by Thy anger, and by Thy wrath are we troubled. Thou hast set our iniquities before Thee, our secret sins in the light of Thy countenance" (Psa. xc. 7). Man was not meant to suffer; man was not meant to die. He was meant to live for ever, blessed beyond thought, in the fellowship of God; but sin was his undoing, bringing with it its wages, which is death.

These are the three great facts of life which reveal to us alike the urgency and the difficulty of redeeming the time. Life is short; therefore our opportunities are few and passing. Life is sorrowful; therefore we are apt to be discouraged, and to let things drift. Life is sinful ; therefore, if we would redeem the time, we must not only overcome adverse circumstances without, but a far worse enemy, the evil heart of unbelief within. These facts, then, give us our directions how to act.

(1) Because life is sinful *let us quickly learn the lesson of forgiveness.* This is God's first word to us. If we are not forgiven, it is impossible for us to redeem the time. We cannot live one moment aright. We are the enemies of God, and every moment in peril. The one thing needful for us is to " believe on the Lord Jesus Christ, and be saved."

And if we have learned the lesson of forgiveness, we must learn also *the secret of victory.* To redeem the time while sin has dominion over us is impossible. To make the best use of life while we are slaves is impossible. We must be made free men if we are to do God the service He seeks of our hand. The man who has not learned to trust Christ as his sanctification wastes the greater part of his life in ineffectual struggles against the forces of sin within him.

(2) Because life is sorrowful *let us quickly learn the secret of God's peace.* To those who visit among the poor it is a familiar truth that their poverty and trouble lie at the root of their idleness and thriftlessness. The man who feels that by the hardest work he can perform he can only make himself a little more comfortable than by doing nothing is apt to think that his comfort may be too dearly bought. If we are to redeem the time, we

must be saved from discouragement. Worry is one of the greatest wasters of time as well as of strength that can be named. He who is kept by the peace of God will do infinitely more work and better work than the man whose mind is worried and distressed. Whatever takes friction out of life increases its working power.

(3) Because life is short *let us learn that every moment of it must be filled.* The two greatest enemies to the right use of our time are idleness and purposelessness. When under the power of the one we do nothing; when under the power of the other we do nothing useful. Now both idleness and waste of time are terribly common. But for them both we may be delivered by a deeper consciousness of God, and of our accountability to Him. Under the guidance of His Spirit we may occupy every moment, and hallow our whole life by a holy intention.

That we may do this, several things are necessary.

The first of these is that we begin the day with God. The importance of the "Morning Watch" cannot be overestimated. We have to pray with the Psalmist, "Cause me to hear Thy loving kindness in the morning" (Psa. cxliii. 8), if we would occupy the day well.

The second is that through the whole day we seek the direction of God. It is not in man that walketh to direct his steps ; and the day is lost in which we seek to do our own will. This was what the holy men of old felt when they prayed so earnestly : "Cause me to know the way in which I should walk, hold up my goings in Thy paths " (Psa. cxliii. 8).

A third necessary thing for a redeemed day is the Divine protection. We are surrounded with enemies who will entrap us and draw us away from God. We need all the day to be hid under the shelter of God's wing.

And the fourth thing necessary is Divine empowerment. When we know God's will we must be taught to *do* it. We must not only be shown the path, but led in it. But if we are Divinely directed, Divinely protected, Divinely empowered, and if from morning to night we carry with us the consciousness of God, then will our days be redeemed. We shall abide in Christ, we shall abound in good works, and when He shall appear, we, by His grace, shall have confidence and not be ashamed before Him at His coming.

CHAPTER X.

THE ASPIRATION AFTER THE SENSE OF DIVINE GUIDANCE.

"Cause me to know the way wherein I should walk" (Psa. cxliii. 8).

In every Christian's heart there is a deep desire to do the will of God. It is of the very essence of regeneration that it implants within the soul a principle of life, which finds its supreme delight in the will of God. But with the desire to do the will of God there comes the desire to know it, and thus the question of guidance becomes one of the most practical of the Christian life. "I am perfectly willing," cries one, "to do the will of God, but my difficulty is in knowing in particular cases what God's will for me is."

That we may receive guidance is beyond doubt. The promises on this subject are innumerable. Our God takes upon Him the name of Shepherd; but one of the first duties of the shepherd is to guide his sheep. In the thirty-second Psalm God promises, "I will guide thee

with Mine eye." In the forty-eighth Psalm we read,
"This God is our God for ever and ever: He will be our
guide even unto death." Isaiah gives us the promise,
"The Lord shall guide thee continually," and Zecharias
tells us that one of the objects of the advent of Christ
was that He might "guide our feet into the way of peace."
Without question, we may receive guidance from God as
to His will.

But ere we go further it may be well to recall the
conditions of guidance. They are set before us in the
twenty-third Psalm. To be guided we must first of all
be among the Lord's sheep. It is those who willingly
follow the Shepherd whom He is able to lead. If we
know not the Shepherd, in guidance we have neither
part nor lot. Then if we are to be guided, we must
know something of *rest of soul*. It is after He has made
His sheep to lie down, that the Shepherd leads them by
the waters of rest. To worry about guidance is the
surest way to lose it. Here is the secret of the failure
of many of God's children to hear His voice. Let us be
at rest, let us be sure that the guidance will be given.
Then we shall be in the best possible condition to receive
it when it comes.

And notice very carefully, it may be given without
our being at all sensible of it. We must distinguish
between guidance and sensible guidance. If we are the
Lord's people, and honestly commit our way to Him, we
shall be guided. But we may have no comfortable sense
of it. We may lay our case before God in all sincerity.
We may ask Him to make His will clear to us, and may
be perfectly whole-hearted in our determination to do
it when it is made clear to us. Yet God may leave us,
even at critical moments in our life's history, without

the smallest gleam of the light we perhaps imagined would come.

In such circumstances, how are we to act ? Surely in faith. God has promised to guide us; we have asked Him to guide us; we are honestly desirous of doing His will; it is therefore our duty to believe that He does guide us, even when we do not feel His guidance. We act to the best of our judgment, and we have the right to believe that behind our judgment there is the Spirit of our Father, leading us according to our prayer to do our Father's will.

But we may not only receive guidance, but be sensible of it. This adds immensely to our comfort. When feeling reinforces faith, we act more joyfully. The Israelites of old were not only guided, but guided by the pillar of cloud and fire. God was with them, and they knew it. Now, what do we read in Isaiah xxx. 21 ? " Thine ears shall hear a word behind thee, saying, This is the way, walk ye in it, when ye turn to the right hand, and when ye turn to the left." Here there is promised not only guidance, but the sense of it. The word is to be heard at each turning-point of the way, discovering the path of the Divine will. Now, what was contained in this promise of the prophet is certainly contained in the promise of our Lord regarding the Holy Spirit. He is to be our guide, making known to us our Father's will.

The conditions on which we receive this sensible guidance are these : —

(1) If we would have sensible guidance, *we must ask for it.* There must be on our part the recognition that we cannot guide ourselves. This is part of that spirit of humility which is so essential at every stage of the

spiritual life. It is the meek that God has promised to guide in judgment; it is the meek to whom He has promised to teach His way. But this meekness means the spirit that distrusts its own wisdom, and looks up to God in prayer. The explanation of the lack of sensible guidance in some lives is that they have never really asked for it.

(2) If we would have sensible guidance, *we must wait for it.* To ask, but not to wait, betokens insincerity in the asking. When we pray God to guide us, we put the matter at issue out of our hands into His; when we act without waiting for guidance, we take it out of God's hands into our own. It were better not to ask for guidance at all, than, having asked, to act without waiting for it. To wait may be exquisitely trying, but it must be done. This is one of the great lessons that we learn from the life of Elijah. He waited at the brook Cherith until it was dry, and did not move until the word of the Lord came to him. Meekness, to which the promise of guidance is made, involves patience as well as humility.

(3) If we would have God's guidance, *we must be ready to act on it without questioning, the moment it is given.* God will not guide a disobedient child, or one who has the slightest intention of being disobedient. If we ask God for guidance, and when he gives it to us refuse to follow it, we become incapable of hearing God's voice until we have confessed our sin, and received cleansing. For God usually guides by whispers, and those who would be guided by Him must keep near Him.

When our Father means to give us very clear indications of His will, He very often makes these three things to occur — His Spirit, His Word, and His Providence. There arises within us a convinction that a certain course

is the right one for us to take; then we find through the
Word some confirmation of this feeling, and straightway
God's providence almost shuts us up to this course. It
is very delightful when this happens. It would happen
much more frequently were we living nearer God than
we are.

Let us give ourselves up to be filled and controlled by
the Spirit. Let us walk in the Spirit, and He will lead
us only in the paths of God's will.

CHAPTER XI.

THE ASPIRATION AFTER THE POWER TO WAIT.

THE value of the grace of patience in the spiritual life
is universally recognized. A high place is given to it in
Scripture, and a high place has always been assigned to
it in the esteem of Christian people. Now, this grace of
patience has two elements in it. The first is *power to
endure*, and the second is *power to wait*. The one has a
relation to suffering, the other a relation to time. The
two elements are separable in thought and experience,
some who have the one being conspicuously lacking in
the other. It is with the second of these that we have
now to do.

The Word of God sets a high value on patience in the
sense of power to wait. It often exhorts to it: " Rest in
the Lord, and wait patiently for Him," cries one (Psa.
xxxvii. 7); " The Lord is a God of judgment, blessed are
all they that wait for Him," says another (Isa. xxx. 18);
while a third says, " It is good that a man both hope and
quietly wait for the salvation of the Lord " (Lam. iii. 26).

This power to wait may be lacking in a character otherwise strong and beautiful. Scripture supplies us with many instances of the lack of it, and of the mischief done for the want of it. It might almost be said that the very fall of man was due to this. Had our first mother Eve only had the power to wait, she would not have snatched at that knowledge which God had for a time denied to man. Haste, as well as unbelief and self-will, was an element leading to that sin which

" Brought death into the world, and all our woe."

In Abraham we have another instance of the same thing. To him the promise of God was given that he should be the father of nations. He believed God, and his faith was accounted to him for righteousness. But, though strong in faith, he was lacking in patience. So he fell in with the plan of his wife Sarah for the procuring of a seed, and laid up for himself and his wife a heavy store of family trouble.

The same impatience appears in Rebekah in connection with the promise made to her favorite son Jacob. Here the results were even more disastrous than in the previous case. In both these cases we have a faith that could lay hold on the Divine promise, without the patience which could wait for God to fulfil His promise in His own way.

I believe that this impatience is at the root of a great deal of the worldliness in the Church of Christ to-day, which we all so much deplore. Men want immediate results, which they can report to the world. They are not content that one should sow and another reap. They are not content with the promise, "My Word shall not return to Me void." They want visible signs of success, ample funds, large communion rolls, crowded churches. And to gain these, some men have gone to the theatre manager, to teach them how to carry on the work of the Church of God.

But while the Bible supplies us with instances of the lack of this grace, it also supplies us with notable instances of its presence. Perhaps the noblest Old Testament case is that of David. Here was a man to whom God had promised the throne of Israel. He believed God. He knew he would be king of Israel. But he would not take the fulfilment of the Divine promise into his own hands. Twice, at Engedi and at the Hill of Hachilah, his relentless foe lay sleeping under the edge of his sword, but he would not touch him. He had the power to wait. He knew that the God who had promised was also able to perform.

But the supreme example is our Blessed Lord Himself. There are few things about the life of our Lord more impressive than His patience. Was there ever a life where there was such temptation to haste? The world was dying around Him. He spent thirty years of His life on earth in almost complete obscurity, and even when He began His work in public, nothing could make Him hurry. When at Cana His mother urges Him to act, He says, " My hour is not yet come." When Martha and Mary would have Him haste to the rescue of their brother, He abides two days in the same place. Our Lord Jesus had this grace of waiting in absolute perfection.

This power to wait has its roots in confidence in God. It is he who believeth, who shall not make haste. Now the faith that gives us patience is a twofold faith. It is, first of all, a faith in God as a God of love. When we are quite sure of this, we become willing to wait, because we know so well that time will vindicate God. In patience we possess our souls. Then it is a faith in our own immortality. We know that God will not only vindicate Himself, *but that we shall see it.* So we are kept quiet.

We shall now seek to discover what will be the attitude of a man's mind toward God, when he has attained it to the grace of patience in this sense. An examination of the various words used for "waiting" throws light on this point.

When a man truly waits *for* God, his attitude is —

(1) An attitude of *Silence.*

In many places in our Bible the words "Wait on the Lord," might be rendered "Be silent unto the Lord." This is the idea presented to us when it is said, "It is good that a man both hope and *quietly wait* for the salvation of the Lord" (Lam. iii. 26).

(2) An attitude of *Devotion.*

In one of the words used for "waiting," the root idea is *to adhere.* This is the word used in that beautiful passage, Isa. lxiv. 4, where we read of the God, "Who worketh for Him that waiteth for Him."

(3) An attitude of *Watchfulness.*

He who is waiting for God to work will have his eyes ever towards the Lord, that he may catch the first signs of his Father's working. He will eagerly study every revelation God has given of his purpose, he will avail himself of every help, seeking to hold himself ready to act whenever God calls him to be a fellow-worker.

(4) An attitude of *Intense Desire.*

One of the words for "wait" comes from a root that means "to writhe as in pain." This shows us that although a man may be content to wait until God acts, he may at the same time be consumed with the desire that God should act at once. He may feel with terrible keenness the need of Divine interference, and may cry out for it, while all the time waiting patiently.

As we close this chapter, let us notice how all these characteristics of true waiting are seen in connection with the great hope of the Church — the coming of our Lord Jesus Christ. For that we are looking. For that we are waiting. And as we wait, what is, or ought to be, our attitude? Surely one of silence, as of those who are listening for the footsteps of the returning Lord. Surely one of devotion, as of those who desire to abide in Him, that when He shall appear they may have confidence, and not be ashamed before Him at His coming. Surely one of watchfulness. Has not the Lord bidden us watch? And will not obedience to His command lead us to treasure and study every hint He has given as to the time when His return may be expected? And, finally, one of intense desire, as of those who have heard the Master say, " Behold, I come quickly "; and answer back with gladness, "Amen, even so, come, Lord Jesus."

CHAPTER XII.

THE ASPIRATION AFTER A COMPLETE LIFE.

" Ye are complete in Him " (Col. ii. 10).

WHAT a glorious fulness of being there is in our God! He is always full-orbed. He is infinite, eternal, and unchangeable in His being, wisdom, power, holiness, justice, goodness, and truth. And the longing for fulness

of life, which is found in every true Christian, is the
mark of his Divine lineage. It is because man is so
great, and has been made in the likeness of God, and by
regeneration become a partaker of the Divine nature, that
he so cries out against the things which narrow and cramp
his life. He who has tasted what communion with God
means, longs to know what is "the fulness of the blessing of the Gospel of Christ." We shall now mention
some of the elements that enter into the life of fulness
of blessing, and then indicate in a word or two the path
which leads to this fulness.

(1) In the complete life there is, first of all, *a fulness
of Faith.*

This is the foundation grace. He that cometh unto
God must believe. Until there is faith, there is no spiritual life at all.

Look at the case of Abraham. Of him the Scripture
expressly says that he died in a good old age, an old
man, and *full.* In his case the aspiration we are dealing
with had been fulfilled. He had lived to have a complete life. But what was the foundation of Abraham's
life ? Was it not faith ? He was the father of the
faithful. He was strong in faith, giving glory to God.
It was the greatness of Abraham's faith that made it
possible for God to raise on it a character of such strength
and beauty. If we would have a complete life, let us
pray daily, "Lord, increase our faith."

(2) In a complete life there is *a fulness of Light.* He
to whom the fulness of the blessing has come has his
eye single, and therefore his whole body is full of light.
He is by the Spirit of God led into the knowledge of
God. God's Word is to him an open book, and he has
an increasing knowledge of, and sympathy with, the

plans and purposes of his Father in heaven. Along
with this he finds himself in possession of a wonderful
knowledge of God's will. He knows by a Divine leading
what God would have him be, and by the impartation of
divine wisdom how God would have him do it. To live
thus in the light, to be thus freed from perplexity and
doubt, is one of the highest privileges of the life of
fulness of blessing.

(3) In a complete life there is *a fulness of Patience.*

How remarkably this was manifested in the life of
Abraham! He had the grace of patience in its two
forms — he had the power to suffer, and the power to
wait. How severely his patience was tried! God made
many promises to Abraham, but Abraham must have
thought God took long to fulfil them. Think what a
trial of patience the continued barrenness of Sarah must
have been. It was such a trial that the patience of
Abraham at last gave way under it, and in the matter
of Hagar he tried to take the fulfiling of the Divine
promises into his own hands. Now, where the life is
full of blessing, the Spirit of God works such confidence
in our God that we possess a patience entirely super-
natural.

(4) In a complete life there is *a fulness of Grace.*

He who has entered into fulness of blessing has a
courtesy and gentleness, a humility and tenderness about
him which is most attractive. There is a wonderful
civilizing and ennobling power about the grace of God.
When it takes possession of a man, it greatly modifies,
if it does not remove, the roughnesses and rudenesses
of his character. It clothes him in the beauty of the
Lord. It gives him that consideration for others, which
is the very foundation of good breeding. In all the great

saints this graciousness is found. We find it in Abraham's treatment of the children of Heth, in David's treatment of Saul, and it is conspicuous in every action of the life of Paul the Apostle. And these were only followers of Him in whom all true grace of character was found in absolute perfection.

(5) In a complete life there is a wonderful *fulness of Brotherly Love*. This is a grace of superlative importance. He who has not learned to love the brethren with a pure heart fervently has yet to learn what the fulness of the blessing of the Gospel is. He whose religion does not make him kinder, more loving, more willing to do helpful things, had better give his religion up, for it is certainly not the religion of Jesus Christ. To this grace of kindness and helpfulness, our Lord attaches such importance that in the great parable of the Sheep and the Goats He has made the want of it the cause of banishment from the presence of God into the everlasting fire.

(6) But the crowning grace of the life of blessing is that which again and again in the New Testament is called *Love*.

We are told that the three chief graces of the Christian character are faith, hope, love; and the greatest of these is love. Now what is this love which is the copestone of the temple of Christian character? I think it is the life of God in the soul. It is what our Lord spoke of when He said, " If a man love Me, he will keep My words, and My Father will love him, and We will come unto him, and make Our abode with him." The fulness of the blessing of the Gospel of Christ is the fulness of the Holy Spirit. The complete life for which we are longing is the life filled with God. He who is

filled with God is filled with love. For what saith the
Apostle? "God is love: and he that dwelleth in love
dwelleth in God, and God in him" (1 John iv. 16).

Such is the complete life after which we are longing.
A word or two as to the path that leads to it.

If we study the life of Abraham, we shall find that
the path to fulness is through a process of emptying. Of
Abraham we read that he died an old man, and full.
But look at the way God had to lead that man before
this could be written of him. He had first to separate
him from home and kindred, and send him out a stranger
upon the earth. Then He had, in connection with the
strife with Lot, to separate him from the love of earthly
riches; then He had to wean him from all self-will in
the manner of fulfiling His promises. And at last He
had to wean him from God's best gifts. When Abraham
laid Isaac on the altar, and raised the knife that was to
make his life an utter desolation; when he was cut off
from everything on earth, and driven back on God alone,
when he was thoroughly emptied, then it was that God
poured into his life the very fullest blessing God Himself
could give. "By Myself have I sworn, because thou hast
done this thing, that in blessing I will bless thee, and in
thy seed shall all the nations of the earth be blessed."

By the same path of utter emptying must we reach
the life of fulness. If God comes to strip us of all that
makes life rich, let us not shrink from His hand. For
the hand that empties is the hand that will fill unto all
the fulness of God.

> "Take us, Lord, Oh, take us truly,
> Mind, and heart, and soul, and will;
> Empty us and cleanse us throughly,
> Then with all Thy fulness fill."